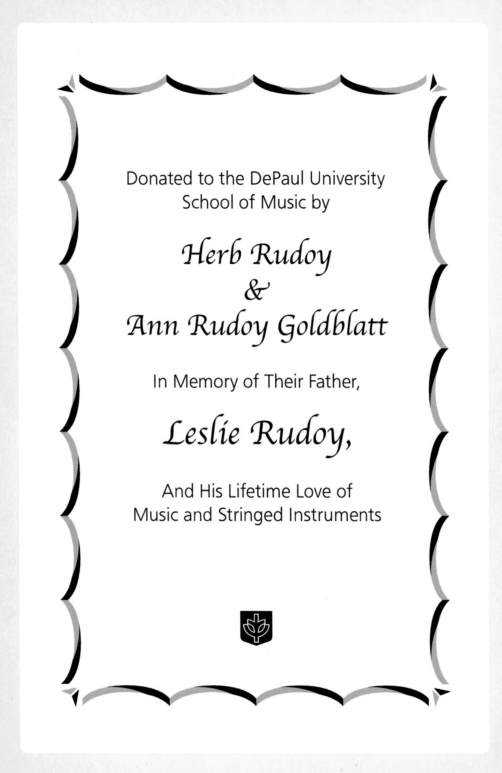

Donated to the DePaul University
School of Music by

Herb Rudoy
&
Ann Rudoy Goldblatt

In Memory of Their Father,

Leslie Rudoy,

And His Lifetime Love of
Music and Stringed Instruments

THE VIOLIN-MAKERS OF THE LOW COUNTRIES

To the memory of my father, Paul Max Möller,
(1875 — 1948)
this book is dedicated.
Further, to all those makers of musical instruments
who, through their arduous and inspired work in the
modest retirement of their workshops, have erected a
lasting cultural monument to the Low Countries.

THE VIOLIN-MAKERS OF THE
LOW COUNTRIES

(Belgium and Holland)

BY

Max Möller

AMSTERDAM

MAX MÖLLER N.V. Violin-Makers and Experts

15, WILLEMSPARKWEG

1955

INTRODUCTION

In 1938, when "Italiaansche Vioolbouw" ("Italian Violin-making") which I had written in close co-operation with my Father, was published, the idea occurred to me to write books on the violin-makers of other countries as well. The violin-makers of the Low Countries deserve the interest of violin-lovers the world over, and the present publication would, therefore, seem to serve a definite purpose.

I have discussed the works of Dutch as well as Belgian violin-makers, since the art of violin-making in the Northern Low Countries shows a remarkable similarity to that in the South.

The information, required to write this book — information which I gladly place at the disposal of my colleagues and others who are interested in violin-making — has come to me from my daily contact with instruments of old, Dutch and Belgian masters, as well as from repeatedly scrutinising and photographing important parts, and from repairing and owning famous instruments, myself.

I have, furthermore, reproduced numerous detailed, life-sized photographs of violins. This is the first publication of its kind in which this method has been adopted. I sincerely hope that certain characteristics will become more familiar to the reader from these reproductions than from any verbal description. I also hope that in this way violin-makers will be able to find the models which they so badly need. If this publication were to help the violin-makers of the Low Countries to find and develop a new, individual style, inspired by their famous, national predecessors, I shall feel amply rewarded for all the work spent on photographing and reproducing all the life-sized details. Whilst writing this book, I have drawn some valuable information concerning dates of birth and death of certain makers from Dirk J. Balfoort's well-known register "De Hollandsche Vioolmakers" ("The Dutch Violin-makers") which was published in 1931 by H. J. Paris, of Amsterdam. A number of violin-makers, registered in that publication, will not be found in this book. It has been my aim to mention only those who excelled in the art of violin-making.

As is the case in every Art, it is essential also in violin-making for a certain period to pass after the creation of an instrument, before its merits can be judged objectively. This is why I have not listed the violin-makers who are still active, and only mentioned in passing those who are carrying on the workshop of a deceased violin-maker.

If this book will stimulate the general interest in the so important art of violin-making in the Low Countries, my aim will have been achieved.

MAX MÜLLER

Amsterdam, April, 1955

THE VIOLIN-MAKERS OF THE LOW COUNTRIES

The works which in the course of time have been published on the history of violin-making, and especially von Lügtendorff's book which was written with great assiduity, but which, alas, must now be regarded as obsolescent since it was published more than 30 years ago, give a chronological survey of the different nationalities (Part I), as well as an alphabetical register (Part II). When looking closely at both parts which, during all those years have been used by violin connoisseurs, one finds that Part I usually is in good condition, whereas Part II, more often than not, shows marked signs of frequent handling. One is, apparently, interested in names, and much less so in the chronological order of events and in the manner in which the various violin-makers, in centuries past, have influenced one another. Often enough, one hardly knows where certain authors have lived and worked. Little consideration is, therefore, given to the influence which other local arts may have had on violin-making.

That the art of violin-making has reached great heights in many places where, for instance, in old times the art of painting had attained an outstandingly high level, is certainly no mere coincidence. In Italy, I recall towns, such as: - Cremona, Venice, Florence; in France: - Nancy and Paris; in England: - London, mainly; and also in the Low Countries, where Amsterdam, the Hague, Antwerp and Brussels should be mentioned.

It will always be necessary to regard the art of violin-making within the framework of other creative arts in order to obtain a clear insight in its true essence and development.

As early as the 15th century, violin-makers of Antwerp used to be made members of the Guild of St. Luke. The old Antwerp School of painting is so world-famous that there appears to be no need to commemorate here some of the great names of that period. Like-wise, Antwerp's architecture, dating from the early 17th century, has gained world-wide fame. Small wonder that such surroundings formed the ideal setting for the inspiration of, and a market for, outstanding artists, also in the field of violin-making.

Furthermore, it should not be forgotten that both Antwerp and Amsterdam have always been at the cross-roads of an intensive, international traffic. This facet, too, has always been promotive of a busy exchange and development of all arts.

13

If I commence my survey with the early 17th century period, I do this in order to remain as concise as possible. Of course, violin-makers have lived and worked in the Low Countries before that period, but to date so little of their works is still known that that period appears not worth discussing. Moreover, the artists used to concentrate rather on making lutes, but hardly made any violins.

It is a pity that numerous makers of the more primitive instruments, made about 1470, with which, for example, the wood-carver van den Bosch portrays one of his "Musicerende Engelen" ("Angels, making music"), never used to sign their instruments, so that we cannot even guess their names. Furthermore, we know from experience that in those days attempts at restoring instruments which had got broken, were rare, so that most instruments were fairly soon lost to later generations.

Furthermore, it should be remembered that in countries like, for instance, the Netherlands, one is "blessed" with that seldom abating desire to spring-clean, with the result that many ancient works of art were sooner lost here than in those countries where one was more attached to old things. This, undoubtedly, partly accounts for the fact that many more of the works of the early Italians have been preserved than of the early Dutchmen and Belgians. I do not believe that the latter were any less productive than their Italian contemporaries.

Ever since the beginning of the 17th century, Antwerp and Amsterdam, towns of great similarity, have housed the grand-masters of violin-making of the Low Countries. Amongst the greatest Dutchmen were Jan Boumeester, Hendrik Jacobs, Pieter Rombouts, Willem van der Sijde, Cornelis Kleynman. Surely, it was a matter of course that in the Netherlands of the Golden Age, when almost all branches of art attained outstanding heights, the town of Amsterdam offered a prosperous existence, also to those great violin-makers. Antwerp, Amsterdam's big rival in those days, was the place of residence of the violin-makers Matthijs Hofmans and J. B. van der Staghmeulen. The old Antwerp masters were, perhaps, numerically inferior to their Amsterdam colleagues, but the quality of their art was certainly not second to that of their Northern neighbours.

It is a remarkable fact that in the Netherlands, in the early 17th century, the art of violin-making was centralised in Amsterdam. It was not until the middle of the Golden Age that violin-makers of artistic standing began to take up residence in other towns. In Belgium, in those days, on the other hand, makers of the same standing as their Antwerp and Amsterdam colleagues could also be found in other towns. I mention Willems, of Ghent; Snoeck, of Brussels.

All the masters, mentioned so far, used to follow practically the same style in their work, viz. Amati's style, but their interpretations were so individual that one certainly cannot say that all they did was copying the old master. Where they received their training, is a mystery. I do not believe that they ever went to Italy, as so many painters and architects of that period had done. Yet they could hardly have acquired that refinement of technique that is apparent in their work through self-training. I am rather inclined to believe that perhaps one of the numerous Italian violin-makers has once upon a time come to the Low Countries and trained a pupil. In the same way, it often happened in those days that Italian violinists and composers came to our countries to have their music printed.

Furthermore, within the framework of the guilds it was considered of paramount importance to have received one's training under a master, so that members of the Guild of St. Luke, of Antwerp, must have learned the art from others, and — this goes without saying — the Italians came foremost as skilled craftsmen and artists in violin-making.

I am also convinced that a close contact must have existed between the old Antwerp and Amsterdam masters of violin-making, because of the great similarity of style as well as of technique. Like the old Amsterdam violin-makers, Hofmans (Antwerp) and Willems (Ghent) frequently used whalebone for their purfling. Another notable point of similarity between the old Amsterdam and the old Antwerp masters was their usage of red wood, instead of spruce for the tops of their instruments.

I venture to contradict what historians have said about varnish, namely that the early Flemish and Dutch with their varnish approached the Italians more closely than any other nationality. Whilst I have the utmost admiration and reverence for the magnificent varnish used by those old masters, it must be revealed that varnish of practically identical composition was used by contemporaries of other countries. (In France: - Claude Pierray; in England: - Barak Norman; in Germany: - Joachim Tielke.) One may even go as far as saying that prior to 1730, bad varnish was non-existent!

In noting that prior to 1700 or, to be exact, prior to 1720 only "Italianising" violin-makers worked in the Low Countries, we must not overlook the fact that, in those days, all Italian arts were held in high esteem. Italian music was in great demand, and from numerous Italian works on architecture, published in Amsterdam, with illustrations which spoke for themselves, even without translated notes, the admiration for that country was abundantly obvious.

In all objectivity it may be stated that the 17th century Antwerp and Amsterdam violin-makers are justly considered, throughout the world, to be the biggest rivals of the famous Italian "luthiers". Their work constitutes a memorable contribution to the esteem in which so many arts of the Low Countries are held.

THE 18th CENTURY

The undisputed strivings of *French Art* are mainly reflected in the 18th century period. In the Netherlands, everything French is then the height of fashion, especially in architecture. In violin-making the same taste is followed. It is most remarkable that in this period the centre of violin-making has, in Belgium, moved from Antwerp to Brussels and in the Netherlands, from Amsterdam to the Hague. These new centres constituted the high-spots of the newly adopted French style of living in the Low Countries. It is difficult to say whether or not this new, French-inspired period in violin-making meant a decline of that art.

Until 1737, the great Antonio of Cremona worked in a style which, until about 1780, was ignored by violin-makers outside Italy. Whilst Nicola Amati was eagerly followed by non-Italians, it was going to take our violin-makers many more years before they began to understand Stradivarius' conception which broke with so many traditions.

Pieter Rombouts worked, until 1740 — although in the latter period of his life he produced very little — in a style which might be described as boldly interpretative of Amati. This description of his work would appear more correct to me than to describe his style as Stainer-inspired, as some historians would have it.

When contemplating the work of Rombout's contemporary, J. B. Lefebvre who, judging by his name at any rate, must have been of French origin, the turning point in Netherlands violin-making in this transition period from the 17th to the 18th century becomes only too discernible. There is no Italian influence to speak of, at least not of Amati or Stradivarius. Lefebvre's conception may possibly have been indirectly inspired by the Gaglianos who, after the death of Stradivarius, became the leading suppliers of instruments for the Italian musicians. I mean to say that, perhaps, traces of 18th century Italian style (particularly of the Naples school) are apparent in the French instruments of Guersan, Benoist Fleury and contemporaries, but that Lefebvre must have been inspired mainly by the latters' style.

In this period, one is definitely seeking a different sound target; one aims at a bigger tone at the expense of the quality of the sound. It is worth noting how quickly one adjusts oneself to a certain tone for string instruments. It is, therefore, a matter of course that in the 18th century, in France and in the Low Countries the Gagliano style is adopted for tone. A different kind of varnish is required, one which is harder and which helps to create a louder and more penetrating tone. This type of varnish dries more quickly and is easier to handle.

One has the impression that, already in this period, the violin-maker is compelled to devote much of his time to repairing old instruments and that he, therefore, tries to gain time for making new instruments, particularly by using more quickly drying varnishes. Furthermore, he very likely had to reserve some time for dealing in old instruments — a handicap which is felt even more by our present-day violin-makers. This is apparent from the elegant label which we have spotted in some instruments and which reads: - "Werd verkogt bij Gosewijn Spijker" ("Sold by Gosewijn Spijker"). This highly-talented violin-maker must have done some considerable trading, for otherwise, there would have been no need for him to have these beautifully etched sale-tickets printed.

No doubt, the products of the 18th century violin-makers of the Low Countries are extremely good musical instruments, but one cannot escape the impression of a certain decline when comparing them with instruments of the preceding period.

Again, the art of violin-making does not stand alone in this respect. Architecture of the same period is, likewise, much less varied than that of the 17th century. Hardly any monumental churches were built and far fewer impressive civic buildings were erected. And again, like in contemporary violin-making, many patrician houses of 17th century origin were rebuilt and modernised. The 18th century Dutch violin-makers no longer give us the beautiful warm colours of Jacobs and his contemporaries; instead, we find a more placid yellow which, as stated before, strongly resembles the work of the Frenchman Guersan and, in certain respects, that of the Gaglianos of Italy. In Brussels, Joseph Benoît Boussu (creative period ± 1740 — ± 1780) works in the same style; he may be regarded as the "chef d'école" of the Belgian School of that period.

The best-known Dutch masters of that century are, no doubt, Johannes Cuypers and his sons Johannes Theodorus and Johannes Franciscus, whose works are discussed in detail in the alphabetical register.

THE 19th CENTURY

Whereas the 18th century constituted a period of comparatively large productivity among the violin-makers of the Low Countries, the 19th century is marked by a noticeable decline. The fact that a well-made violin has an almost unlimited term of life, resulted in a vast number of instruments from the two preceding centuries remaining in use, so that musicians were able to acquire such instruments without having to go to 19th century violin-makers for new ones.

Moreover, at the time of the death of Cuypers Senior (1828), our country was already being swamped with cheap violins, made by home industries (centres of violin-making in France and Germany).

J. B. Vuillaume, of France, together with his numerous assistants and pupils, must not be overlooked. He was highly productive and it may well be said that his workshop alone was practically capable of meeting the demand for new, better-class instruments of the whole of Europe of that period!

Apart from Pressenda and Rocca, Italy of that same period brings us few violin-makers of standing.

It is France that makes Belgium and the Netherlands reap the benefit of its tradition in violin-making. We find Nicolas François Vuillaume in Brussels; Georges Mougenot went to live and work at Liège; the Heynbergs and Bernards who are still at work in that same town, established a style and tradition of their own. Grandjon and Louis Bernardel bring the French style of the period to the Netherlands and initiate the Kok brothers in their working method. The latter, by the way, succeeded in giving their personal interpretation of that style.

Occasionally, we are able to spot a rekindling of past glory, for instance in the work of Cornelis Weel (Utrecht 1809—1871), when he is at his best.

It is, perhaps, useful, within the general framework, to revert for a moment to J. B. Vuillaume. In spite of due feelings of respect for his amazing energy and productiveness, it should be realised that he has had a most detrimental influence on the creation of individual works of art by violin-makers. It was mainly he who discovered a means to overcome the 19th century distaste for new instruments and who started to make mostly instruments which had the appearance of being old. This introduced imitation into the art of violin-making. Of course, the connoisseur is able to recognise J. B. Vuillaume's touch.

19

Vuillaume himself has never attempted to sell his instruments to the world as old, original instruments. The fact remains that a violin which has been made without cheating, i.e. without artifices to make the varnish appear old, becomes much more beautiful through usage than an instrument which has been made to appear old from the start. Furthermore, due to the flow of instruments, purposely made to look old, from J. B. Vuillaume's workshop, the distaste for "new violins" is stimulated.

The violin-makers refrain more and more from making new instruments and, disappointed, they remain servile to music by restricting themselves to repairing the innumerable old instruments in use amongst musicians.

THE 20th CENTURY

At this stage, it is perhaps too early yet to give a synopsis of the 20th century development in violin-making.

In all arts, this century is, no doubt, one of endless probing, of the ever apparent desire to create a style of one's own. Unfortunately, in the majority of cases, decennaries are required before one can determine what may be retained and what has been a definite mistake in the development.

It is unfair to criticize, here and now, any expression of any creative art whatsoever, unless we have had sufficient time since the manifestation of such expression to give us an objective view.

In the early 20th century, we find a curious admiration for technique, i.e. for manual dexterity in making violins.

One sees now violin-makers in the Low Countries who produce instruments with a painfully correct finish. This technique was made particularly popular by Eugen Gärtner, of Stuttgart, and is called "Gärtnerism". In our country, it is Johann Stüber who became an enthusiastic follower of Gärtner; recently, however, he has developed a more personal style. In Belgium, Gärtner's style is traceable in the work of Hilaire Darche, a violin-maker of standing.

The classic ideal of violin-making is spirit and taste first and then workmanship. In this period, however, workmanship and manual dexterity are first and foremost, at the expense of taste. A well-trained and experienced hand has always been necessary in violin-making, but unless that hand is guided by a cultured mind, its works will lack that seducing charm which alone makes them a true Work of Art.

Many makers who had a highly spiritual taste, but who, in some respects, were lacking in manual dexterity (Joseph Guarneri "del Gesu"), are, quite rightly, far more appreciated than that other category of violin-makers who sacrificed everything to a overcorrect finish of their instruments.

In Amsterdam, Max Möller I is very active. His ideal is to work after the Italian style, with strong, personal interpretations. Thanks to his great many good instruments, he is able to arouse a taste for new instruments in the Netherlands. His son and pupil, Max Möller II, who has had his training under the Italian master Sacconi, and under Charles Enel and Amédée Dieudonné of France, attempts to realise a new style which aims at combining the Italian, French and Dutch traditions.

In Liège, a centre of Belgian contemporary violin-making, the Bernards and Heynbergs are creating instruments which combine the best French traditions with a rising Belgian national character of this art.

In the present period, when the values of innumerable things which formerly used to be taken for granted, are doubted, the traditions of violin-making inevitably are from time to time subjected to doubtful questioning.

There are, however, certain accepted facts that can never be denied. The period in which technique was the highest ideal, can be regarded as closed. The making of new violins must be stimulated; one should aim at supplying a sufficient number of instruments to replace — possibly in the future — old instruments which prove to be irreparable. In order to achieve that aim, Government subsidies to violin-makers who are in need, will be found to be less effective than the magnificent initiative which has resulted in the Hendrik Jacobs Contest at the Hague, or the Violin-Makers' Contest at Liège. It is only on such occasions, that the public will have the opportunity to compare a reasonable number of works from contemporary violin-makers. When reproaching the modern violin-makers with deficient productiveness, the public should remember in the first place that only a wide-spread interest provides a fruitful stimulant for any artist. In this connection, attention is called to the fairly large production of violas nowadays, in the Low Countries. This is due to the interest which the younger generation of viola players has shown in new instruments which are adapted to prevailing demands. It need not be different where violins and celli are concerned. These days, high-grade instruments are made which can meet any demands, made by the musicians. Not all violin-makers of the Low Countries have the capability and the impulsive spirit which are required for the creation of a work of art, but there are a few.

Some warning would appear appropriate at this point. In the field of violin-making little consistent literature exists; it is there that dilettantism in its worst form is frequently found and the danger of indulgence in extravagances is ever imminent.

When a dilettante is introduced to the public with great clamour, he will often, albeit only temporarily, be hailed as a new genius of violin-making, but — and this cannot be said with sufficient emphasis — he will always exert a detrimental influence on the reputation and the well-being of the properly trained and artistic violin-makers.

Once the public's healthy and warm interest in new instruments has been roused, the violin-makers of the Low Countries are bound to prove, also in the future, that they are worthy to carry on the great tradition of their predecessors.

Hendrik Aerninck, Leyden, 1684, Viola

Max Möller

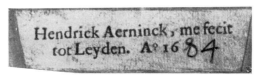

Hendrik Aerninck, Leyden, 1684, Viola   Max Möller

Erhard Amman, The Hague, 1749   Max Möller

Erhard Amman, The Hague, 1749   Max Möller

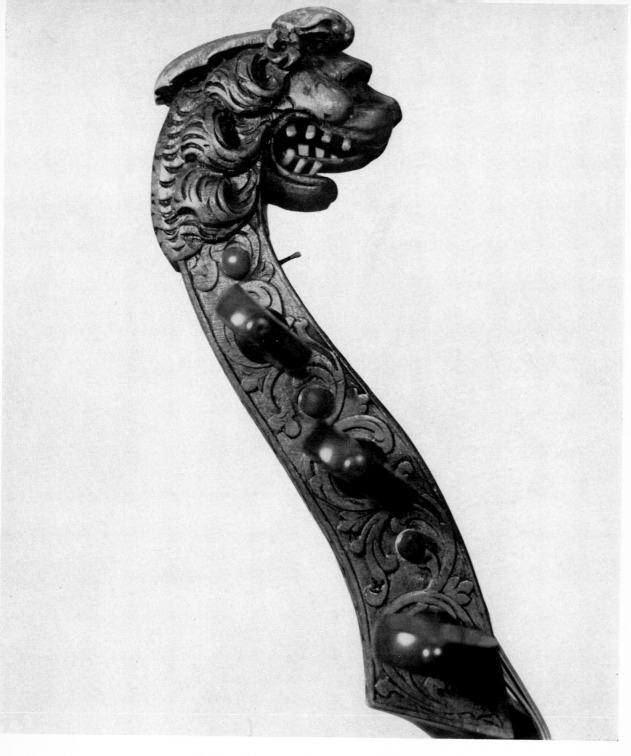

Pieter Bochs, Amsterdam, 1625, Viola da Gamba,   Mr. Johan Wagemaker

Jan Boumeester, Amsterdam, 1683   Municipal Museum, the Hague

Joseph Benoît Boussu, Brussels, Period 1755, Viola   Mr. Leo Blom

Joseph Benoît Boussu, Brussels, period 1750   ex Max Möller

„Repaired by L. Bernardel"

Ambroise de Comble, Tournay, 1752, 'Cello   Max Möller

Ambroise de Comble, Tournay, 1752, 'Cello   Max Möller

Johannes Cuypers, The Hague, period 1760, Viola

Mr. Szymon Goldberg
ex Max Möller

Johannes Cuypers,
the Hague, 1766

ex Max Möller

Johannes Cuypers, the Hague, Period 1770, 'cello　　　　ex Max Möller

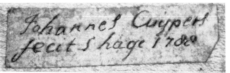

Johannes Cuypers, The Hague, 1783   Max Möller

Johannes Cuypers, the Hague, 1796

ex Max Möller

Municipal Museum, the Hague   Max Möller

Johannes Cuypers, The Hague, period 1790, Kits

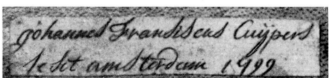

Johannes Franciscus Cuypers, Amsterdam, 1799

Mr. D. van Wezel
ex Max Möller

Johannes Bernardus Cuypers, The Hague, 1808   Max Möller

Hilaire Darche, Brussels, 1901

H. Driessen, Nijmegen, 1809   Max Möller

H. G. Duwaer, Utrecht
1886—1887

Mr. L. Duwaer
ex Max Möller

J. B. le Febvre, Amsterdam, 1767

ex Max Möller

J. B. le Febvre, Amsterdam, 1772, 'cello   Municipal Museum, the Hague

J. B. le Febvre, Amsterdam, period 1750, Viola

Mr. R. Legger
ex Max Möller

Antwerp, period 1690
Matthijs Hofmans,

Mr. C. J. Steeman
ex Max Möller

Matthijs Hofmans, Antwerp, period 1690   Max Möller

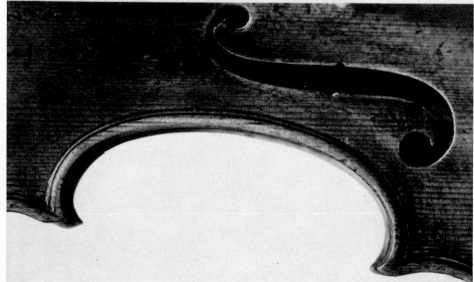

Hendrik Jacobs,
Amsterdam, period 1670

Mrs. Luyten-Werker
ex Max Möller

Hendrik Jacobs,
Amsterdam, period 1670

Max Möller

Hendrik Jacobsz, Period 1693

Dr W. F. H. Brunet de Rochebrune
ex Max Möller

Hendrik Jacobs, Amsterdam, period 1695   Mr. Johann Stüber

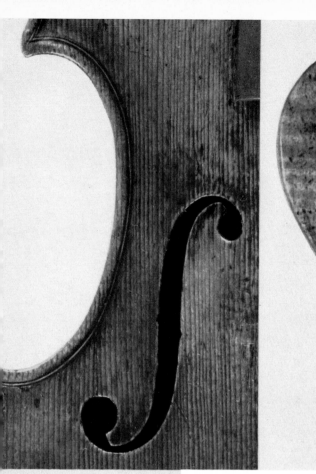
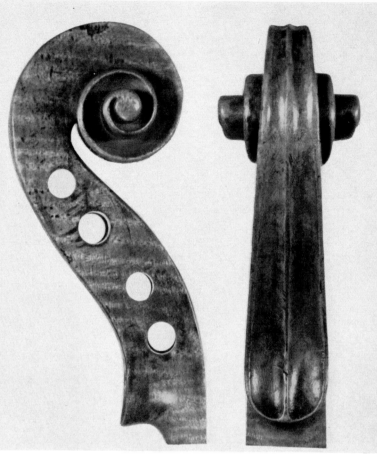

Cornelis Kleynman, Amsterdam, 1685   Rembert Wurlitzer

Cornelis Kleynman, Amsterdam, 1685

Rembert Wurlitzer

Kok Brothers, Amsterdam, period 1850   Max Möller

Christian Lechlytner
me fecit Leyden A°. 17

Christian Lechlytner, Leyden, period 1790, Viola

Municipal Museum, The Hague

Max Möller,
Amsterdam, 1915

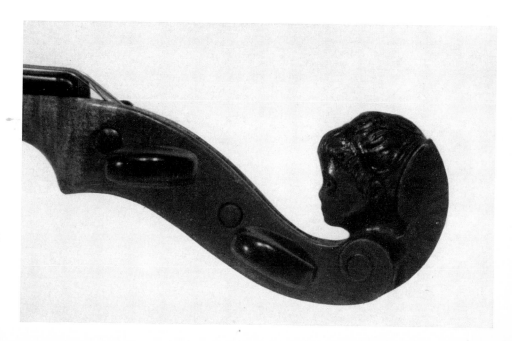

Max Möller, Amsterdam 1913   Mrs. Noordzij

Max Möller, Amsterdam, 1934

Max Möller, Amsterdam 1943

Pieter Rombouts, Amsterdam, 1722, 'cello

Mr. L. Schreuder
ex Max Möller

Pieter Rombouts,
Amsterdam, 1722,

Mr. L. Schreuder
ex Max Möller

Pieter Rombouts, Amsterdam
Municipal Museum, the Hague

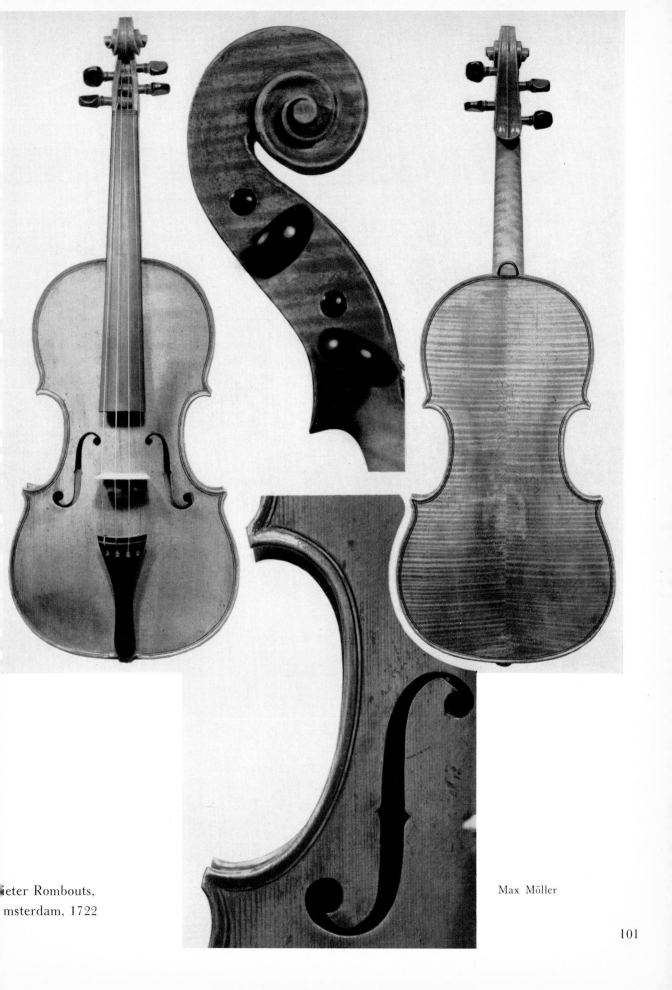

eter Rombouts,
msterdam, 1722

Max Möller

Pieter Rombouts, Amsterdam, 1708, Viola da Gamba   Municipal Museum, the Hague

Joannes Arnoldus Roumen,
Amsterdam, period 1840

Max Möller

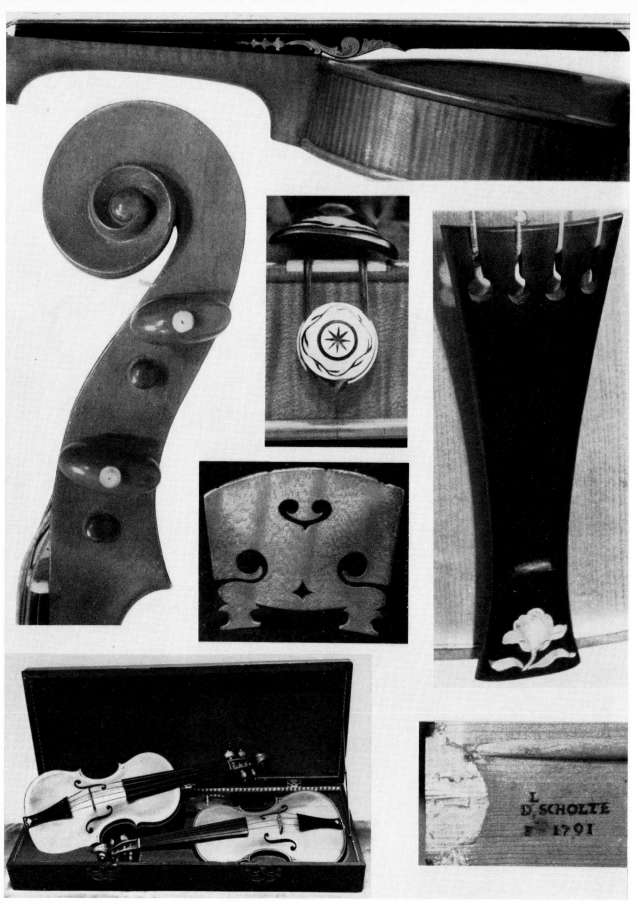

D. L. Scholte, Amsterdam, 1791

Mr. Sam Swaap

Gosewijn Spijker, Amsterdam, 1760, Viola   ex Max Möller

„Sold by Gosewijn Spyker"

Gosewijn Spijker, Amsterdam, 1760, Viola   ex Max Möller

Willem van der Sijde, Amsterdam, 1694

Dreesmann Collection
ex Max Möller

Willem van der Sijde, Amsterdam, period 1700

Mr. R. Rhodius
ex Max Möller

Willem van der Sijde. Amsterdam, period 1700

Mr. W. G. Hofker
ex Max Möller

Nicolas François Vuillaume, Brussels, 1867

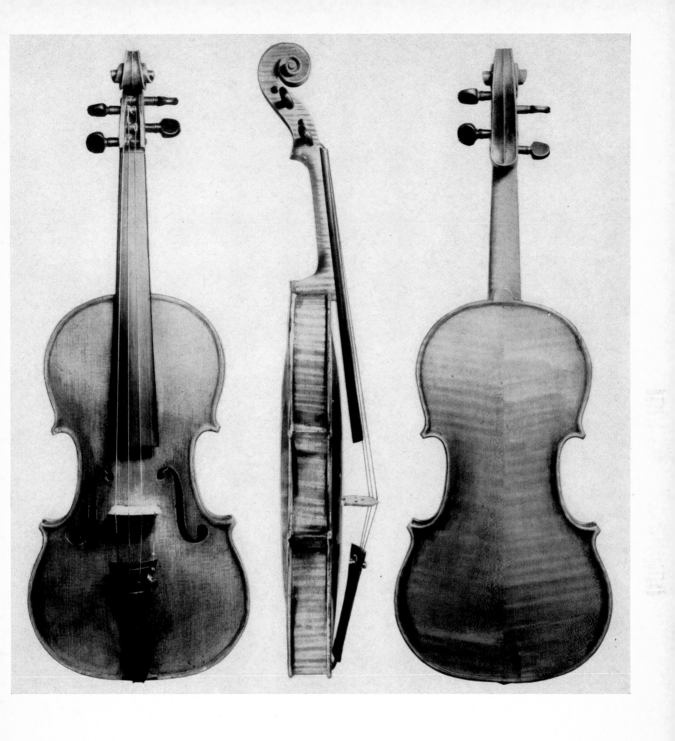

Nicolas François Vuillaume, Brussels, 1866

Mr H. J. Jung
ex Max Möller

Jean Baptiste Wattier
the Hague, 1733

Johann Stüber

Cornelis Weel, Utrecht, 1858   Max Möller

Cornelis Weel, Utrecht, period 1850, 'cello

Dr. W. Kraak

Eugène Eberle, Rotterdam, 1885—1936

Emile Heynberg, Liège, 1864—1939

ALPHABETICAL REGISTER
OF THE
VIOLIN-MAKERS OF THE LOW COUNTRIES

AERNINCK, Hendrik. 1649 — after 1701 (Leyden, Holland)

The work of this violin-maker who originated from Quakenburg, West-phalia, shows a perfect assimilation to that of his Dutch contemporaries; an elegantly shaped instrument with long corners and well-made sound-holes. His work bears the signs of thorough training. His varnish is beautiful and of a soft composition. In one respect only, one might call his finish somewhat deficient, viz. the purfling of top and back of instruments of his that I have seen, has only been traced on. A noteworthy circumstance is that practically without exception, he used to trace double rows of purfling.

The instrument, registered and discussed by Balfoort, is a specimen which is little representative of its maker; the instrument was severely damaged by repairs to which the author refers in his book.
According to von Lütgendorff, there were two violin-makers of the same name. That information seems to be incorrect. Aerninck's works may sometimes resemble those of Willems, of Ghent, but there is certainly little truth in his saying that Aerninck's style is similar to that of Cuypers.

AMMAN, Erhard. About 1720 — about 1770.

Of this violin-maker, some excellent instruments which had been made at the Hague, have passed through my hands. One might perhaps describe his style as one lying between the refined conception and finish of earlier Netherlands violin-makers and the somewhat heavier construction of later Dutchmen.
Chronologically too, he fits into this transitory stage. His work, however, is by no means untidy or technically deficient. His purfling is always of whale-bone; the shape is bold and wide; the corners are not as long as those of many other Dutch violins. One might call his style distinctly inspired by Carlo Bergonzi's works of ± 1740; it is quite striking to see a maker follow this great Cremonese maker so closely, in a period when the latter was not yet so greatly admired as he is now!
Amman's varnish leaves little room for improvement; it is perhaps harder of composition than that of Jacobs and his predecessors. His scrolls are well-carved and full of character, another reminder of the great Carlo Bergonzi.

Doring, humorously, states in his magazine "Violins" (ed. September-October 1950) that — according to von Lütgendorff who admits that he does not know any of Amman's works — this violin-maker is accepted as a very good one.

BERNARD

Family of Liège "luthiers". The oldest member is André Bernard, born in 1869. At the age of fourteen, as an apprentice, he enters the workshop of Gand & Bernardel, of Paris, where he remains for five years. Later he has his own workshop in Liège, at the Boulevard de la Souvenière. In 1918, he moves to 9 rue St. Paul. He has been awarded numerous distinctions and was, in 1954, Honorary President of the "Concours International de Quatuor." His son, Joseph Bernard (1911—1940), has, ever since his youth, been his father's pupil. In 1930, he was awarded the Gold Medal at the International Exhibition in Liège, when he was still a boy. It is most regrettable that this very promising violin-maker died at the early age of 28.

André Bernard's second son, Jacques Bernard (1919—   ), succesfully carries on his father's workshop and is, besides, keenly interested in reconstructing primitive instruments, such as viols, clavichords etc.

Furthermore, we are indebted to him for a remarkable musicological collection which he himself has brought together and which he keeps open to the public.

BERNARDEL, Louis. About 1806 — 1847.

One of the very few French violin-makers who have worked in Holland. It is not known at whose instigation he came to Amsterdam in 1836. The establishment of a violin-maker's workshop in that city which, at that time, was starved of "luthiers", was no luxury. His style of work does not deviate from the usual style of Mirecourt in the early 19th century. His technique is very good, but it lacks personality and charm.

After his death in 1847, his widow induced Jules Joseph Grandjon to carry on her late husband's workshop. Grandjon was also a native of Mirecourt. It is, at any rate, to Louis Bernardel's credit to have taught Johan Warnaar and Gerrit Kok, both of Amsterdam, the art of violin-making.

BOCHS, Pieter. 1578 — 1656.

An Amsterdam violin-maker who mainly made viola da gambas, one of which is owned by Mr. J. Wagemaker. It is a pity that this instrument has lost its old varnish through repairs and that other repairs have caused this instrument to lose also its original character.

From my father's personal notes, made around 1900, it is apparent that he had come across several of Bochs' viola da gambas which still had the beautiful varnish of the old Amsterdam maker.

BORBON, Caspar. Brussels, about 1650 — 1700.

Together with van der Staghmeulen, this violin-maker is one of the few "luthiers" of the Low Countries who worked after the Brescian style. He was very little productive. His father, Pierre Borbon, who also worked in Brussels, in the first half of the 17th century, has produced even less.

BOUMEESTER, Jan. Amsterdam, 1629 — 1681.

This outstanding violin-maker is to be regarded as one of the best representatives of the Dutch School. He was born in the same year as Hendrik Jacobs and raised the art of violin-making in the Low Countries to soaring heights. He was clearly inspired by Nicola Amati, but never copied him blindly.

In my opinion, Boumeester's design of the sound-holes which are, as a rule, more open, accentuates his difference in style from Jacobs. His purfling, always of whalebone, is inserted a little more inside the instrument's outer edge. The channel around the outline of top and back shows a hand which has been trained to the extreme. His entire work is that of the skilled artist. The only detail which creates an impression of lesser elegance, is in the scroll, the button of which seems to be a little massive.

His varnish, sometimes clear yellow, then again profoundly dark red, is always of the most beautifully soft composition and sometimes with a "craquelé", like some famous Italian instruments. At the Municipal Museum at the Hague, there is an instrument of his on show which is entirely in its original state, with the old neck: - a gem of old-Dutch violin-making.

Balfoort states that Boumeester's instruments remind one of the work of Hieronymus Amati, without saying, however, which of the two violin-makers of that name.
Von Lütgendorff writes that Boumeester's work may easily be mistaken for that of Pietro Guarneri, of Mantua. His work, however, shows such obvious personality that the trained eye of the expert will always spot it without fail. Having frequently compared the works of these violin-makers with one another, I cannot but conclude that Boumeester's work was mainly inspired by Nicola Amati.

BOUSSU, Joseph Benoît. Middle and late 18th century.

This Brussels violin-maker worked in a style which shows great similarity to the early work of Cuypers. Boussu's instruments are sometimes a little high-arched. His sound-holes are very erect and their upper and lower openings are fairly large. His purfling is beautifully inserted and follows the instrument's outline far into its corners. His varnish is, like Cuypers', always yellow to light brown. The scrolls of his instruments, and particularly of his violas, show an interesting detail, in that the coils end up in a very big, massive looking button. Furthermore, the scrolls are strongly hollowed out along the sides. These remarkable violas have an excellent shape (16½″ in length of body).

Boussu used, in addition to a very small label, also a brand "Boussu", usually on the inside of the back of the instrument, practically in the centre.

Both Von Lütgendorff and Vannes, speak of a style "after Amati". In my opinion, it would be better to describe his style as inspired by the Frenchman Guersan and Benoist Fleury.

BROCHE, Marcus.

Pseudonym for Marc Snoeck. See under Snoeck.

COMBLE, DE, Ambroise. Latter half of 18th century.

This well-known Flemish violin-maker, who worked at Tournay, made instruments of entirely individual style. The eye is immediately struck by the very low position of his sound-holes. This creates the impression as though the upper part of the tops of his instruments is proportionately bigger than their lower section. His work is marked by sound training and artistic finish. His scrolls are beautifully carved, with small, elegant curves and narrow peg-box. The purfling is refined and inlaid with great care. His varnish is of very good quality and — characteristic of his period — sometimes a little hard, after the style of Guersan, and at other times of softer composition, like in the case of his great Flemish predecessors.

Apart from violins, this maker also made violas and celli of excellent quality. Characteristic of the latter are frequently the flat backs of the scrolls.

Von Lütgendorff accuses this violin-maker of inexactitude in his work, in my opinion undeservedly. He also states that De Comble's tops are often yellow whilst the other parts of his instruments are red. From the above description of his work, however, it is evident that De Comble was a great artist and it is hard to believe that he would ever resort to cheap extravagances.

CUYPERS Johannes Theodorus. 1724 — 1808.

Known as Johannes Cuypers.

Perhaps the most productive of all Dutch violin-makers. It has always been my aim to discover who may have been this maker's teacher. He is frequently said to have worked after "a Stradivarius model". This should be interpreted that he worked more after Stradivarius than after Amati. The more I was able to compare the works of Cuypers, particularly his rare, early ones, with those of his contemporaries, the more I came to believe that he must have had his training in France, either under Guersan, or under Benoist-Fleury. Balfoort quotes an article from G. H. Broekhuizen in "Caecilia" (1847) in which the writer stated that Cuypers went to Paris as a carpenter and there was taught by Guersan to make violins, as he was unable to find employment. Balfoort denies this possibility, but I see no reason why Broekhuizen's statement which was made with positiveness, shortly after Cuypers' death, should not be correct.

Cuypers' earlier works, prior to 1775, show remarkable refinement; purfling which follows fairly long corners right up to the end; small, elegant scrolls. In this early period, Cuypers made more celli and violas than later on, all of high-grade quality. In those early days he used printed labels which are far less known than his handwritten ones of later years. Also as regards his material, he is far more dainty than later on. For his tops he uses fine-grained spruce and they are made in two parts. In later years, however, Cuypers appears to have had a tremendous stock of spruce which allowed him to make his tops in one single piece. (This stock of wood was so big that it lasted his sons right up till 1840).

Furthermore, in this early period, his F-holes have a very particular shape, vide the cello (page 47) and violin (page 45). The heads, however, already are of that very vertical design which will remain a characteristic throughout Cuypers' later periods. The backs of the heads are quite flat, like in later years.

The viola (page 43) is rather typical of his very early period and has, for a long time, been regarded as a work by Gosewijn Spijker, a Dutch maker and contemporary of Cuypers, although it originally bore a label of Amati (!) I am proud to have been able to establish its identity after I had handled quite a few of Cuypers' instruments with printed labels and found their characteristics identical to those of this viola. It will now foster the name of these early Cuypers instruments all over the world, in the hands of its new owner, Szymon Goldberg.

The somewhat heavy touch apparent in Cuypers' later works in due, I think, to the fact that he made two of his sons participate in the work. This might also explain the circumstance that specimens of his later work are less rare than his earlier instruments. Johannes Franciscus was 14 years old in 1780. In the old days, this used to be an age at which many violin-makers already used to be at work in their fathers' or teachers' workshops.

Johannes Cuypers actually deserves bigger fame as an artist than is bestowed upon him on account of his numerous later works. The instruments which date from the period when his sons were too young to participate, show the conception and finish of the true artist.

In 1795, Cuypers' youngest son, Johannes Bernardus, was at an age that he might have assisted his father, and it is my belief that it was this son who set-in Cuypers' "heaviest" period. Perhaps, Cuypers was aware of it himself and, for that very reason, took to using labels, stating his age, as some sort of excuse.

Owing to his sons' assistance, Johannes Cuypers has been very productive indeed, and he is, in general, foremost in one's thoughts when the Dutch art of violin-making is discussed. That is why outside the Netherlands the somewhat discreditable impression was created of a rather too solid conception of violin-making of the old Dutch makers. Particularly of his later works, a vast number are still known to this day. Of recent years, however, one is beginning to show greater appreciation of his instruments which, generally, meet modern demands for a bigger tone.

An interesting characteristic of Johannes Cuypers' style in this later period is his tops, usually in one piece of wood, without the centre joint which is more orthodox. The scrolls are long drawn; the peg-box is only slightly curved; little finish to their backs. Another interesting detail is the small hole in the scroll button, probably caused by Cuyper's habit to use a pin in order to steady the model of the scroll when tracing it onto the wood.

CUYPERS, Johannes Franciscus. 1766 — 1828.

Johannes Cuypers' eldest, violin-making son who for a considerable period worked in Amsterdam, contrary to his father and brothers who always worked at the Hague.

His work may be distinguished from that of his father's by the somewhat longer mitres of the purfling. For the rest, in conception and execution, it differs little or not at all from old Cuypers' later period.

Von Lütgendorff states that, in his opinion, he must have received his training in Italy, without, however, stating his reasons for that conclusion. He does not support his statement with any complimentary remarks on the work of this artist.

CUYPERS, Johannes Bernardus. 1781 — 1840.

Johannes Cuypers' youngest son. His work shows great similarity to that of his father's late period, but it may be recognised by sharper roundings of top and back.

CUYPERS, Johannes Franciscus II.

Johannes Bernardus Cuypers' son. He has made very few instruments.

DARCHE

A well-known family of violin-makers, originally from Mirecourt, who worked in Brussels from 1854, when Joseph Darche (born in 1825) started working in N.F. Vuillaume's workshop. Joseph sent his son Hilaire back to Mirecourt to learn the art of violin-making there, among others from Charles Gaillard. Hilaire also worked under N. F. Vuillaume in Brussels for some time, and then associated with his brother, a piano-maker, under the name of Darche Frères. Hilaire Darche's instruments received more recognition abroad than the works of other members of the Darche family. He displays an extremely refined technique in his work; so much so, in fact, that personality of conception is sometimes sacrificed to the excellent workmanship. The tone of his instruments is extremely big. He died in 1929.
Yet a third Darche worked under Vuillaume: - Charles François (1820—1874). Paul Darche (1846—1881) concentrated almost exclusively on repairing violins.

This family still counted some more violin-makers, but as they did not work in the Low Countries, I shall not enlarge upon their work.

DECOMBLE, see COMBLE, de.

DRIESSEN, H. Nijmegen. Early 19th century.

Several interesting specimens of his work have passed through my hands.

138

The shape seldom varies and reminds one Cuypers; so does his entire finish. Only, his sound-holes are longer. The scroll is carved with great accuracy. His varnish, perhaps a little hard of texture, is of a light chestnut-brown. The tone is very satisfactory.

DUWAER, Herman Gerardus. Utrecht, 1842 — 1909.

A remarkable Dutch maker of the late 19th — early 20th century, when there were very few violin-makers in the Netherlands. His entire conception is strongly individual, perhaps somewhat lacking in elegance, but quite bold and flowing in execution. Varnish also deserves appreciation. Very good tone.

EBERLE, Eugène. Rotterdam, 1885 — 1936.

This violin-maker started his apprenticeship, like so many other "luthiers", at an extremely early age, under Charles Ferenczy Tomasowsky, of Hungarian birth, who worked at the Hague.
His actual mentor was Otto Möckel, of Berlin, who had a great influence on his development. His work, like that of his teacher, shows great technical perfection which, however, never causes detriment to his conception. The varnish deserves special mention; it is of a beautiful, transparent yellow. As son of a musician, he devoted careful attention to the acoustic qualities of his instruments.
Engène Eberlé II carries on his father's workshop. He is a violin-maker of equally excellent training. (He also worked under Otto Möckel). His work bears the signs of good taste and culture. In 1954, he was a member of the jury at the International Contest for Violin-makers at Liège.

FEBRE, le, see Lefebvre.

GAMBON, Andries. Maastricht, 1757 — 1846.

The work of this violin-maker is clearly influenced by the Belgian School. Authentic works of this maker, known to me, display a shape which is strongly reminiscent of Matthijs Hofmans. They have the same large upper-sections which are characteristic of the style of Hofmans, a fairly narrow waist and elegantly curved sound-holes. The varnish is of excellent composition. Only in his corners, he cannot quite match the magnificent style of Hofmans.

GRANDJON, Jules Joseph. 1824 — 1900.

A violin-maker from Mirecourt who, having received his training there, worked for a number of years (until 1850) in Amsterdam. His work is clean and of an excellent technique, but it does not differ from that of his Mirecourt contemporaries.

HAKKERT, Jacob Wolfgang, 1891 — 1942.

This violin-maker, who originated from Rotterdam, died tragically during the German occupation. Trained under Didier, of Mattaincourt (near Mirecourt) and worked in the workshops of several outstanding violin-makers in Europe. He was "Luthier du Conservatoire" of Rotterdam and gained recognition as a maker of strings.

HEEFKEN, Johannes. 1728 — about 1780.

The instruments of this maker, known to me, are made after the style of Cuypers' early period. Although his work bears the signs of a well-developed technique, he does not rank among the great violin-makers.

HEYNBERG.

Family of violin-makers, working at Liège. Originally, the family name was Heinsbergen or Einsbergen, from Schiedam. About 1830, at the time of the separation of Belgium from Holland, the name is changed to Heynberg. The grandfather of the present Georges Heynberg was professor of the violin at the Liège Conservatoire. He had the honour to be the first professor to

Eugène Ysaye, idol of Belgian violin playing. After six months, this Désiré Heynberg dismissed young Ysaye from his class with the following comment: - "This child is so super-vivacious and wanton that I have to dismiss him from my class, because he lacks violonistic disposition."

My colleague, Georges Heynberg, to whom I am indebted for this most interesting anecdote, adds: - "The further artistic career of this brilliant virtuoso was bound to give a singular dementi to this, my grandfather's statement." If I add that the two Marsicks (Armand and Martin) have also been pupils of Désiré Heynberg's (1831—1897), it will be readily admitted that the violin-makers of this family have come from an outstandingly musical milieu.

HEYNBERG, Emile. 1864 — 1939.

Began to work in Liège in 1895. Before that, he had his training from Georges Mougenot, of Brussels, and from Gand and Bernardel, of Paris. His instruments which are of high merit, are made after Guarneri del Gésù and the Messias Stradivarius. Finely finished workmanship, with great technical merits.

Heynberg, Georges, (1901 — ....) Emile's son and pupil, is carrying on the paternal workshop with great success. He has been awarded high distinctions. In 1930, he was third out of 71 competitors at the Concours International de Sonorité at Brussels, and in 1954, he was a member of the Jury of the International Violin-Making Contest at Liège.

HOFMANS, Matthijs. Middle and end of 17th century.

This Antwerp violin-maker may certainly be called the greatest of the old, Belgian craftsmen. His work deserves the highest praise. The shape of his instruments is of well-nigh inimitable elegance.

What strikes the eye in particular, are the upper and lower parts which are rounded off to an extreme and which end up towards the middle bouts in very long, narrow corners.

The C's cave in strongly, which gives his instruments an extra light touch. The purfling penetrates deeply into the corners and is inlaid immediately inside the edges of top and back of the instrument. The sound-holes are erect and beautifully curved. His varnish is of excellent quality, always rich in colour and of a beautifully soft composition.

Unfortunately, but few works which bear the original signature of this master-maker, are known today. His hand, however, is quite discernible for experts who have made a study of his works.

In my opinion, his working period is usually timed too late. Judging by the style of his work, I think there is ample justification to fix that period at from 1650 till about 1680.

Von Lütgendorff states that later investigators — however, without mentioning any names, unfortunately — have found that there have been two violin-makers of the name of Matthijs Hofmans; one from 1660 until 1691, and the other one from 1700 until 1725. No works of another Matthijs Hofmans, however, are known to me.

Vannes is most objective in his description of the skill of his great countryman and merely states him to be "un des meilleurs luthiers flamands". He, too, places Hofman's working period rather late, end 17th century, early 18th century.

HOOF, Alphons van. 1878 — 1936.

This violin-maker, who was born at Tilburg, travelled to Markneukirchen in his youth to learn the craft, returned to his native place and settled in Antwerp in 1907. From 1915 till 1920, he worked at Bois-le-Duc where he was patronised by the manufacturer Azijnman. Van Hoof made a number of instruments after a Storioni, owned by this lover of violins. He is an interesting violin-maker with a sound technique.

His son, Antoine van Hoof, born in 1901, is successfully carrying on his father's tradition. He has his workshop at Antwerp.

JACOBS, Hendrik. 1629 or 1630 — 1699.

This violin-maker ranks among the greatest of the 17th century Dutch makers, like Jan Boumeester, Pieter Rombouts, Willem van der Sijde and Cornelis Kleynman.

In this maker's work, we can distinguish between three periods.

The first period, until about 1670, during which he made instruments which might be described as his "perfect Amati type". By comparison, the only points in his disfavour would be the arching towards the centre of the top which dips a little too steeply at the edges, and the fact that his sound-holes are a little too wide as compared with the delicateness of the rest of his conception.

The second period, from about 1670—1685, shows a somewhat bolder style and execution.

142

The third and last period, from 1685 until his death, I would describe as his "Rombouts period". He was at that time about 60 years old, and it is evident that having Pieter Rombouts who became his stepson in 1676 and who was 18 years old of age in 1685, so near, he left a considerable part of the work to be done by this young and talented violin-maker. His instruments of this period show distinct Rombouts features — a rather wide purfling, inserted further than usual from the instruments' contours; the backs of the heads widening considerably towards the lower end.

Without exception, Jacobs' violins, regardless of their period, deserve the highest praise and the varnish is always of most excellent quality.

It is often stated that this maker must have spent some time in Italy. It is my firm belief, however, that neither Jacobs, nor any of the early Dutch violin-makers, have ever been to Italy for their training, but that their knowledge of the Italian style was principally gained from Italian instruments which had been brought to the Netherlands. As for their varnish, I consider it only fair and just to state that the same type for which the early Dutch are famous, has, besides by the Italians, also been used by others, like Barak Norman (English), Jacob Stainer (German), Claude Pierray (French).

It is sometimes thought to be a reflection on the knowledge of experts and dealers alike, that some of Jacobs' works have, at times, passed for Amatis. I have in my time handled several violins of Jacobs which had never been opened before and which bore Amati labels, doubtlessly placed there by Jacobs personally. I firmly believe that, like members of the Klotz family and other followers of Amati, Jacobs had merely intended to indicate that he did not work after his own model, but after the model of that greatly admired violin-maker.

I have never seen a Jacobs instrument which had been thought or certified by a qualified expert to be an Italian instrument. The rumour that many of Jacobs' violins have at some time or other passed for genuine Amatis, is grossly exaggerated and stems from reports from would-be experts.

Photographs taken of genuine specimens, distinctly show the different periods in Jacobs' work; they obviously do not portray Amati characteristics such as are apparent in later works by clever imitators. What I want to point out is that any Amati features are, as a rule, exaggerated in Jacobs' instruments: - longer corners and rather too rounded sound-holes; all strongly individual characteristics of a truly fine violin-maker and not of one who merely copies the work of others.

Some further explanation of Jacobs' labels would seem called for. If reproduced by earlier writers, usually the one dated 1693, is shown. In this book, the second type, dated 1704, is printed. Upon close examination, this ticket is definitely produced with a block, made by the same engraver who had produced Rombouts' labels (compare label, dated 1722). How can Jacobs possibly have had a block made in or after 1700, if he died in 1699? (The last two figures have, as usual, been added in writing to the first two printed ones on the labels). In my opinion, Rombouts must have inherited a large number of instruments, made by his stepfather, and — out of reverence for the deceased — removed the Amati labels which Jacobs had used originally, and replaced them by labels, bearing the real maker's name and the date of the year that he inserted them. It is unfortunate that he omitted to mention the correct dates, but perhaps Rombouts considered such dates of no importance. The 1693 type may have been used by Jacobs personally whenever he did not use an Amati ticket.

KLEYNMAN, Cornelis. Late 17th century, early 18th century.

This excellent early Amsterdam violin-maker deserves to be mentioned in one breath with Jacobs, Rombouts and Boumeester. I have seen samples of this master's work which clearly show that he not only equals Jacobs, but frequently even surpasses him. The workmanship is impeccable and the varnish of his instruments is of the finest, lustrous red, golden yellow or brown.

Doring states the following: — "The writer is in full agreement with Mr. Möller in rating Kleynman in a class beyond comparison. An exquisite example is pictured. It is an instrument of extreme beauty, both as regards shape and the handsome material employed, the two-piece back being made of the choicest wood like that which is found in the finest works of Italian makers. Every detail of workmanship is carried out to a high degree of nicety and the golden varnish is of a fine, rich quality."

KOK, Johan Warnaar (1819 — 1889) and Gerrit (1828 — 1899).

Known as "Gebroeders Kok" (Kok Brothers).
These Amsterdam violin-makers trained under Louis Bernardel and Jules Joseph Grandjon. They made a fairly large number of violins of elegant shape, showing good workmanship. Long corners and usually a yellow varnish of reasonably good composition. After the death of Gerrit Kok, their workshop was carried on by Paul Kunze, of Markneukirchen (born in 1875) who now works at the Hague, a fine and productive maker.
Eventually, the workshop was carried on by Johannes Peereboom who was well-known in Amsterdam as a skilled repairer. He died in 1946 at the age of 68.

Neither von Lütgendorff, nor Balfoort, nor Vannes have mentioned Johannes Peereboom in their latest editions. He was a sincere craftsman of high morals, and I feel proud to commemorate him.

144

KRUMBHOLZ, Lorenz. 1886 — 1944.

This violin-maker originates from Austria. He had his training under Otto Möckel in Berlin, and came to Holland, like many of his colleagues, to Karel van der Meer. Later, he worked under Vedral and finally started his own workshop at the Hague.

Krumbholz was an excellently trained violin-maker who worked after the style of Möckel's, but who was able to acquire an individual cachet. Technically, no fault can be found with his work. His varnish, too, is of good quality. In addition to the instruments, made in his own style, he has also made some good copies, especially after Scarampella.

Of late, his workshop has been carried on by Lorand Racz who displays a similarly fine technical skill as Krumbholz.

LAURENT, Emile. 1854 — 1914.

This Frenchman from Mirecourt received an excellent training there, among others from Auguste Darte who was one of J. B. Vuillaume's well-known assistants. He also worked under Joseph Hell, of Lille, and settled in Brussels about 1900. With such a background and training, it is not surprising that his works show excellent finish. His instruments are made in the French style, typical of his period, after Stradivarius and Guarneri del Gesu. They are technically perfect and have a big tone.

Von Lütgendorff states that Laurent was born in 1859, but that, I suppose, was a printing error.

LECHLEITNER, Christian. 1758/1759 — 1821.

This violin-maker from the Tyrol settled at Leyden at an early age. He made violins and particularly violas which remind one of Cuypers, and in many respects also of Lefebvre. His conception is a little heavy, but technically well-executed. His varnish is identical to that of Cuypers, nearly always yellow and rather hard of composition.

Von Lütgendorff states that he worked after Stradivarius or after Amati, and that his later works remind one of Hendrik Jacobs. Neither my father, nor I, have ever seen instruments of Lechleitner's other than those which remind one of the style of Cuypers. His work is so like that of Cuypers and Lefebvre that I dare to contradict earlier statements to the effect that his style is "very German".

LEFEBVRE, Jacques B. About 1701 — after 1772.

This violin-maker who, from 1725 onward, worked in Amsterdam, probably originated from France.

It is possible that Pieter Rombouts — of whom hardly any instruments are known to date later than 1727 — no longer worked at that time, or very little. Lefebvre, therefore, found ample opportunity to work here, as is apparent from the numerous instruments which he made.

His instruments are quite well-made. Characteristic are his short corners which look a little blunt in comparison with those of earlier Dutch makers. His scrolls are full of character; the chamfers remarkably sharp. It is this maker who influenced other Dutchmen of that time and, strangely enough, in spite of the fact that Rombouts used his superior varnish until his death in 1740, we find that his Dutch contemporaries follow the general style of that period of employing a rather less attractive varnish, typical of 18th century French violin-makers and also of those in the Netherlands of Cuypers' period.

Until Lefebvre, Dutch violin-makers used without exception whalebone purfling. I would here emphasize this statement which contradicts much wrong information from earlier authors. Lefebvre was the first violin-maker in the Netherlands to use wood for the black strips. Works of his alternatingly have whalebone and wood purfling. In my opinion, Lefebvre was not superior to his French contemporaries. His work is rather neat and delicate of detail, with small heads and sound-holes.

LEON, Christian.

Name of a violin-maker who worked at Liège in the years 1870—1890. The Bernards have told me, that his family name is not known. He deserves recognition for the fact that he initiated André Bernard in the art of violin-making and also for having devoted his talents to the musical life of Liège for years on end, at a time when that town was deprived of violin-makers.

Vannes states that Léon was this maker's surname, and that his Christian names were Jean-Pierre.

MEER, Karel van der. 1862 — 1932.

Although Karel van der Meer was not solely a violin-maker, he nevertheless gained a reputation, for during the years 1890 to about 1915, when little or no activity in this field prevailed in the Netherlands, he kept an important workshop going which benefited by his knowledge as a violinist and violin teacher. He knew how to inspire skilled violin- and bow-makers. Many a foreign violin-maker who, later, settled in our country, had been brought to Holland by him. Amongst those was my father, Max Möller who for many years was his "chef d'atelier".

Van der Meer won recognition on account of many violins and violas made in his workshop, but also on account of the many bows, the best ones of which were made by the Frenchman Auguste Toussaint, from Mirecourt.

MEER, Karel van der. 1890 — 1954.

The former's son, who was a violoncellist of note, likewise took an interest in violin-making.

MÖLLER, Max. 1875 — 1948.

Born at Markneukirchen (Saxony), he finds employment in the Nürnberger shops at the age of fourteen, at the same time studying theory at the School of Violin-making. Three years later, Möller enters into a partnership with Heinrich Theodor Heberlein. In 1899, Möller leaves Markneukirchen in order to work with Max Möckel at St. Petersburg. In 1904, he leaves Russia and joins Karel van der Meer, of Amsterdam, with whom he works until 1913, when he opens his own workshop in the Dutch capital.

In addition to being a violin-maker, Max Möller also used to make bows, thus following in the tradition of his earlier principal van der Meer who was also a prominent bow-maker.

Möller's work can be classed in different periods. From 1913 to 1918, he devotes nearly all his time to making new instruments. They are well-made, after Italian examples with the heads sometimes carved to represent women's or angels' heads.

In later years, he gathered the finest collection of old instruments, ever brought to Holland.

Between 1925 and 1929, he concentrates once more on making new instruments and turns his back on the trade in old violins and all that goes with it. In this very productive period, he has gathered quite a number of assistants around him.

From 1930 to 1935, on numerous trips abroad, he once again collects remarkable instruments for Holland.

From 1935 onward, at the age of sixty, he returns to the making of new instruments. This period lasts until his death in 1948. In this last period, he creates 14 large violas which are of outstanding merit, in addition to numerous violins and violoncellos.

In all objectivity, it may be said not only that no other Dutch "luthier" has been as productive as Max Möller, but also that of hardly no other Dutch violin-maker so many instruments are being played by musicians.

It is Möller who created and stimulated the taste in Holland for the well-made new instrument.

Max Möller II, son of the former, received his early training from his father. He studied at the School of Violin-making at Mittenwald, under Charles Enel, Amédée Dieudonné and Fernando Simone Sacconi. In 1935 he went into partnership with his father and finally took over his father's workshop. He received many distinctions, e.g. in 1937, the silver medal "Per Benemerenza" at Cremona. He was a member of the Jury at the Hendrik Jacobs Contest in 1948, as well as at the Italian Contest of Violin-makers in Rome in 1952. He won one of the three Awards of Honour which were issued on the occasion of the Festival of Britain in 1953. In 1954, he received the "Coupe du Gouvernement Provincial de Liège", "avec grande distinction" at the International Contest of Violin-makers.

MOUGENOT, Georges. 1843 — 1937.

A French violin-maker from Mirecourt. For the sake of curiosity, I place on record that he is, as far as I know, the only violin-maker to attain a more advanced age than Stradivarius who died at the age of 93.

Mougenot started his training as a youth under Georges Deroux and moved to Liège at the age of fifteen. He also worked at Aachen after which he returned to Liège until 1875 when he went to work under N. F. Vuillaume, in Brussels.

Mougenot was a very productive violin-maker with all the merits of the 19th century Frenchmen. He had a beautifully skilled hand which enabled him to make instruments of high, technical perfection. As was the custom of that period, he followed the style of Stradivarius and Guarneri, so that, in spite of their technical perfection, his instruments lack personality.

ROMBOUTS, Pieter. 1667 — 1740.

This excellent maker was the son of Sibilla Barents who married Hendrik Jacobs, then a widower, in 1676.

Pieter Rombouts thus became Jacobs' stepson. Dirk Balfoort deserves great merit for having secured this knowledge from his extensive researches through archives. It is clear, therefore, that already at an early age Rombouts must have come into contact with violin-making and assisted his stepfather with his work. Rombouts' assistance becomes particularly apparent in Jacobs work after 1686.

Pieter's hand is heavier, although he was a master at the treatment of the fluting and channelling which runs along the outlines of top and back.

His purfling is wider and, although neatly done, it is rather less delicate than that of Jacobs. His heads also differ from those, made by his teacher, in that they are a little bolder of form. An interesting characteristic of his heads is their narrowness at the tops of the back, widening considerably towards the lower end as is the case with works by de Carcassi brothers.

Rombouts was also an extremely clever maker of cellos which rank among the finest. He appears to have taken a special interest in the production of these instruments. In fact, I would say that I have never seen a cello, attributed to Jacobs, which did not bear ample traces of Rombouts' collaboration. When examining these cellos, one is struck by their extremely wide purfling. Naturally, whalebone is used for the black strips.

The upper and lower sections of the sound-holes, particularly, are remarkable. The heads of these instruments deserve special praise; their backs (the French speak of "coulisse") rank among the finest ever to be seen, and are beautiful of conception, as well as of execution.

One outstandingly beautiful specimen is the cello, referred to by Alfred Hill in his introduction to Balfoort's book which instrument was, at the time, owned by the well-known British collector Ernest Sandeman. At a later date, it was temporarily in possession of W. E. Hill & Sons, changed hands again and was, at one time, owned by me. It is now the property of Mr. L. Schreuder, of Haren.

Some of his cellos' heads are carved in the shape of lions' or satyrs' heads. Those cellos are usually high-arched and not always as finely finished as those which have the usual heads.

Rombouts has also made a number of fine violas and viola da gambas. A beautiful specimen (dated 1708) of the latter is on show at the Municipal Museum at the Hague. Its marvellously preserved light red varnish is particularly striking and reminiscent of the finest early-Italian varnishes.

Of special interest is his label which has not been printed with a wooden block like the labels of the majority of the old masters, but — judging by its outstandingly clear characters — an engraved metal block must have been used. We encounter labels of the same type and characters amongst Jacobs' later works. Of the Dutch masters, Gosewijn Spijker too, used to use an elegantly calligraphed metal block for his labels. Louis Guersan (Paris) and Santo Serafin (Venice) adopted a similar technique for their inscriptions.

Von Lütgendorff's statement that the varnish was "bei aller Leuchtkraft etwas zu dick", would appear slightly biased.

ROUMEN, Lodewich Wilhelm. Late 18th — early 19th century.

The instruments of his hand which I have seen, all date from Amsterdam. Hand-written labels. As a violin-maker, he was by no means inferior to his son whose works are more numerous. When comparing his work with that of Joannes Arnoldus Roumen, I would say that his is a little more elegant; it shows a lighter hand.

ROUMEN, Joannes Arnoldus. 1802 — 1876.

The numerous instruments which I know of this violin-maker, date from his Amsterdam period, like those of his father. They have a very good tone. One might say that they resemble the works of J. B. Guadagnini (Turin period) on account of their rather heavy conception and execution. His varnish reminds one of the later Cuypers.

SCHMIDT, Ernst Albin. 1863—1939.

Born at Markneukirchen, he is another violin-maker whom Karel van der Meer has brought to Amsterdam. Eventually, he started a workshop of his own, here, and became a well-known personality in Amsterdam's musical circles. The numerous violins made by him, are practically all after Guarneri del Gesu and of sound workmanship.
His son, F. W. Schmidt, carried on his father's workshop for some time.

SCHOLTE, B. L. Late 18th — early 19th century.

This Amsterdam violin-maker has produced violins, violas and cellos in fairly large numbers. When examining his work, one cannot help wondering whether he has, perhaps, had training as a carpenter instead of as a violin-maker.
The reason why I mention him here, is that in contrast with the above depreciatory description of his work, the ornamentation of his instruments' finger-boards and tail-pieces is really remarkably good and of excellent taste.

SNOECK.

A family of violin-makers who have been working in Brussels since about 1680. The style of Egidius, the oldest member of this family, is reminiscent of that of Matthijs Hofmans, of Antwerp. Practically the same graceful shape and an excellent technique; perhaps, one might call his archings a little lower than those of Hofmans. Beautiful varnish, not only brown, but often flaming red and soft composition, with sometimes a "crackle finish".

The instruments of his son Marc have less elegant features. His varnish is a little harder, typical for the middle of the 18th century. (He worked from 1720 — about 1765). He uses a pseudonym on some of his labels which read: - "Marcus Broché", besides labels which he signed with his own name. Marc Snoeck's son Henri Augustinus (until shortly before 1800) was very little productive.

SPIJKER Gosewijn. Latter half 18th century.

This excellent old-Amsterdam violin-maker is one of the few who has created really important works in the Netherlands at that time. Apart from a number of violins which bear his name and which have passed through my hands, there are particularly his violas which are, to this day, recognised as of excellent measurements (length of body 16½"). The execution is, sometimes, superior to that of Cuypers at his best. His treatment of details is extremely delicate. He used very good material and a yellow varnish of equally good, soft composition. Fine sound-holes and beautifully inserted purfling.

STAGHMEULEN, Joannes Baptista van der. 17th century.

This contemporary and townsman of the great Hofmans displays outstanding, artistic sense in his work. His instruments are, perhaps, a little less elegant in shape than those of Hofmans, but they betray magnificent personality. A rare characteristic of his work amongst violin-makers of the Low Countries is the ever apparent influence of Brescia. Like other followers of that style, he often decorates his instruments with double rows of purfling and other extra decorations. His varnish is of a beautifully soft composition. It is curious that he used an Italian Christian name. Was he, perhaps, the Antwerp master who had been trained by an Italian or who had Italian relatives?

I disagree with von Lütgendorff's and other authors' statements that his name should really be spelt: "Van der Slaghmeulen".

SIJDE, Willem van der. 1664 — about 1700.

One of the outstanding violin-makers of the old-Amsterdam School. Unlike Jacobs, he was not a follower of Nicola Amati, but had a style of his own. It is a pity that, like in the case of Kleynman, his work is nowadays often mistaken for that of Jacobs. The experienced connoisseur, however, will be able to discern van der Sijde's characteristics at once.

His conception is bolder than that of Jacobs. Corners are a little heavier and the purfling is consequently somewhat wider. His varnish is definitely not inferior to that of Jacobs. The sound-holes are placed close to the purfling. Typical feature of his violins is the rather "flat breast" between the sound-holes. This is quite a deviation from Jacobs' execution of this section of the top. I, personally, greatly appreciate van der Sijde's work, since it is practically not influenced by other makers. He definitely ranks amongst the finest and most individual Dutch makers of the 17th century.

VUILLAUME, Nicolos François. 1802 — 1876.

Known as "Vuillaume de Bruxelles". This outstanding violin-maker, brother of J. B. Vuillaume, settled in Brussels in 1828. Before that, he had had a sound training at Mirecourt and had gained practice under his brother in Paris for many years. Although not so productive as Jean Baptiste Vuillaume, a considerable number of his works have been preserved to this day. One might describe his work as more individual than that of his brother, although he mainly worked after two models, a Stradivarius and a Joseph Guarneri del Gesu. His finish leaves little room for improvement. Fine purfling, inserted with great accuracy. Varnish of good composition. Beautiful tone.

From Vannes' comment that he is mainly known for his copies of the Servais-Stradivarius cello, one might think that his violins are less well-known. From the above description of his work one may conclude that that interpretation is incorrect.

WATTIER, Jean Baptiste. 18the century.

This violin-maker worked at the Hague after the style of Lefebvre. His work bears signs of a strong French influence. The heads have long-drawn peg-boxes near the scroll, a typically French, 18th century characteristic. The body is rather high-arched. Sound-holes are strongly rounded.

An interesting detail is that the tops of his violins, practically always of one piece of wood, have the wide grain at the side of the E-string. This is contrary to the style of other violin-makers who, when making one-piece tops, usually kept the wide grain at the side of the lower strings.

Balfoort registers a violin-maker, J. B. Walther, of the Hague (18th century), stating that all he knows of this maker is that a violin with this man's signature, and dated 1727, was auctioned at the Hague. It is highly probable that a printing error had crept into the auction sales catalogue, or that the label in the instrument had been misread, so that this also was one of Wattier's violins. At any rate, no other works by Walther have become known.

WEEL, Cornelis. 1809 — 1871.

A violin-maker whose best works bear the marks of great old-Dutch traditions. His instruments are rather flatly built; perhaps technically not perfect in appearance, they provide ample compensation in their high degree of good taste and personality.
It is remarkable that this violin-maker has received so little appreciation from earlier authors. I would reveal that I hardly know any other maker of that period who used a finer varnish. Weel's varnish is of superior quality and frequently with a "craquelé" whilst his instruments, on the whole, show a fine, individual conception and are quite "Italian" in character. Particularly his cellos deserve the highest praise.

WILLEMS I, Hendrik. About 1650 — about 1700.

One of the outstanding violin-makers of the Belgian School.
The most productive member of this family of violin-makers who worked at Ghent. His work is clearly inspired by Matthijs Hofmans. It shows signs of outstanding refinement in every respect. Long corners; beautiful purfling; excellent varnish.

WILLEMS II, Hendrik. About 1680 — about 1750.

This violin-maker's work can hardly be distinguished from that of his father's, except that it is somewhat heavier.

GLOSSARY	TERMES TECHNIQUES
Angle of the fingerboard.	renversement, m.
arching	voûte, f.
high-arched	bombé
Back	fond, m.
back in two pieces	fond en deux pièces, m.
one piece back	fond d'une pièce, m.
bass-bar	barre, f. barre d'harmonie, f.
belly, table, top	table, f.
block	tasseau, m.
top-block	tasseau du haut, m.
lower-block	tasseau du bas, m.
corner-block	tasseau du coin, m.
body	coffre, m. corps, m.
length of body	longueur du corps, f.
bow	archet, m.
bridge	chevalet, m.
button, (for attaching tail-piece)	bouton, m. (d'attache de cordier.)
Channel, (of the edge)	gorge, f.
chamfer	chanfrein, m.
cheeks, the (of the head)	les joues, (de la tête) f.
coat of varnish	couche de vernis, m.
curl, figure	onde, f.
figured	ondé
small curl; having a	à ondes serrées, f.
broad curl; having a	à ondes larges, f.
light curl; having a	légèrement ondé
cut on the quarter	coupé sur maille
cut on the slab	coupé à contre sens
Ebony	bois d'ébène, m.
edge	bord, m

FACHAUSDRÜCKE	TECHNISCHE TERMEN
Stachel, m.	punt, de (cello)
F-loch s.	F-gat, het
Griffbrett, s.	toets, de
Flanke, w.	flank, de (van boven- en achterblad)
Schneckengräben, m.	uitwerking van de achterkant van de kop
Hohlkehle, w.	kanaaltje, geultje. (uitholling, ter plaatse v. d. inleg, de omtrek van boven- en achterblad volgend.)
Geige, w. Violine, w.	viool, de
Jahrring, m. engjährig, feinjährig	jaarring, de, draad van hout fijn van draad (-nerf), fijngejaard
breitjährig	breed van draad (-nerf), breedge-jaard.
Grundierung, w. (Lack)	grond, grondlak
Kopf, m.	kop, de
Blättchen, s. Zäpfchen, s.	hieltje, het (hielvormig einde van het achterblad waartegen de greep gelijmd wordt.)
Taschengeige, w.	dansmeesterviooltje, het
Zettel, m.	etiket, het; inschrift, het
Reifchen, s. Gegenzarge, w.	rand-versterking, de; (smalle reepjes hout aan de binnenkant v. d. zij-randen aangebracht.)
Bereifung, w.	binnenwerk, het; (rand-versterking met blokjes.)
Ahorn, m.	esdoorn, (Lat. acer)
Hals, m.	greep, de
F-Kerben, w.	F-keepjes, de; (inkepingen v. h. F-gat die de plaats van de kam aan-geven.)
Sattel, m. Obersattel, m.	kielhoutje, bovenste kielhoutje (stukje ebbenhout aan het boven-einde van de toets.)
Untersattel, m.	onderste kielhoutje.

GLOSSARY	TERMES TECHNIQUES
Peg	cheville, f.
peg-box	cheviller, m.
pine, (wood)	pin, m. (bois de)
plain	uni (sans ondes)
purfling	filets, m.
	filetage, m.
Rib	éclisse, f.
Saddle, bottom nut	sillet du bas, m.
scroll	volute, f.
sound-hole	ouie, f.
sound-post	âme, f.
spruce, (wood)	sapin, m. (bois de)
stained	teinté
overstained	surteinté
stop	diapason m.
Table	table, f.
tail-gut	attache de cordier, f.
tail-piece,	cordier, m.
tail-pin	pique, f.
thickness	épaisseur, f.
tip, (of the head)	bouton (de la volute), m.
top	table, f.
Varnish	vernis, m.
viola	alto, m.
violin	violon, m.
violin-cello	violoncelle, m.
cello	basse.
volute, (see scroll)	volute, f.
Wing	chantau, m.
wing of the F	la patte d'F. f.

FACHAUSDRÜCKE	TECHNISCHE TERMEN
Wirbel, m.	schroef, de
Wirbelkasten, m.	schroevenkastje, het
Fichte, w.	grenehout (Lat. pinus silvestris)
ungeflammt.	effen, ongevlamd
Adern, w.	inleg, de
Einlage, w.	
Zarge, w.	zijrand, de
Sattel, m. (Unter-)	kielhoutje, het onderste (stukje ebbenhout, waarover de lus van het staartstuk loopt)
Schnecke, w.	krul, de
Schallloch, s.	klank-gat, het; F-gat
Stimme, w. Stimmstock, m.	stapel, de
Fichte, (w.) (Fichtenholz)	vurenhout, het, (Lat. picea excelsa)
gebeitzt	gebeitst
verbeitzt.	verbeitst
Mensur, w.	mensuur, de
Decke, w.	bovenblad, het
Henkel-Saite, w.	lus, de
Einhänge-Saite, w.	
Saitenhalter, m.	staartstuk, het
Stachel, m. (Cello)	punt, de (cello)
Stärcke, w.	dikte (van het hout)
Knöpfchen, s. (der Schnecke)	knopje (waarin de laatste winding van de krul uitloopt.)
Decke, w.	bovenblad, het
Lack, m.	lak, de
Bratsche, w.	alt, de; altviool
Violine, w.	viool, de
Violincello, s.	violoncel, de;
Cello, s.	cello, de
Schnecke, w.	krul, de
Flanke, w.	aangezette flank
F-Klappe, w.	F-vleugel, de

LIST OF ILLUSTRATIONS

CONTENTS